My B
Bit

Liz Lewis

Geographical Association

Barnaby Bear
is in bed.

He is thinking about his first day in Skarsvåg.

I went to school with
Andreas and Christian.

Then we climbed up the hill to see the view.

I met Nils. I liked his hat.

...but I liked his reindeer best of all.

Some people in Norway do not like the reindeer because they eat up the plants.

They spoil the gardens
in the village.

Barnaby is very sleepy after thinking so hard, but a funny noise keeps him awake.

He opens the curtain
and peeks out to see.

Barnaby still thinks the reindeer are fantastic.
Don't worry hungry reindeer - I won't tell!